The Good Shepherd

Retold by Philip Turner
Illustrated by Bunshu Iguchi

J.M. Dent & Sons Ltd
London & Melbourne

This is my family. It is called a flock. How many sheep are there? The old ones say there are a hundred and that the Shepherd knows each one of us by name.

The Shepherd calls me Benjamin, because I am
the smallest and the youngest. I am still only a
lamb, but the Shepherd cares for us all, both
old and young.

The carrion crow frightened me so much that I fell in the river. I thought I would drown, but the Shepherd came to my rescue. He warned me of crows and water, and told me to beware of danger.

This is the valley where I was born. It grew brown and dry, and there was not enough to eat. The old ones said the Shepherd would lead us far away to green places.

It was a long, long way and the track was stony.
I became very tired, but did not stop since it
would have been dangerous to be left behind.

The Shepherd led us to this beautiful
valley where the pasture was green, the
grass sweet, and there were many
flowers. It was a good place to be —

a good place to kick up my heels,
to run away from the flock, to play
by myself. But I forgot . . .

. . . I forgot what the Shepherd had said about the danger of straying. I looked and looked, but there was no one to see. I called and called, but no one answered. I was all alone, except for the circling crow.

It grew dark and cold. I hid under a rock and thought of the flock and the Shepherd. I felt very lonely and very afraid.

In the starlit night I heard a voice calling, "Benjamin! Benjamin!"

As the moon came out, the Shepherd found me and carried me home. It was warm and safe on his shoulder, and I fell asleep.

I woke to find the flock surrounding me,
bleating and baaing because they were glad
to see me safe. I was happy to be home with
them and the Shepherd.

BUNSHU

The story of the Good Shepherd is one of the parables Jesus told a long time ago.

"If one of you has a hundred sheep, and loses one of them, does he not leave the ninety-nine in the open pasture and go after the missing one until he has found it? How delighted he is then! He lifts it on to his shoulders, and home he goes to call his friends and neighbours together. "Rejoice with me," he cries. "I have found my lost sheep."

Luke 15:4

First published in Great Britain 1986
Illustrations © Bunshu Iguchi 1985
Japanese Text © Takeshi Sakuma
English text © J.M. Dent & Sons Ltd 1986
Illustrations originally published in Japan by Shiko-Sha Co Ltd

Phototypeset in 18/23pt Plantin
by Tradespools Limited, Frome, Somerset, England
Printed in Japan
for J.M. Dent & Sons Ltd
Aldine House, 33 Welbeck Street, London W1M 8LX

British Library Cataloguing in Publication Data

Turner, Philip
  The good shepherd.
  I. Title   II. Iguchi, Bunshu
  823'.914[J]   PZ7

ISBN 0-460-06245-X